· 1045 ·

Don't forget that we are ultimately
judged by what we give,
not by what we get.

· 1046 ·

Never complain
about the music in someone else's car
when you're a passenger.

· 1047 ·

Read Tom Peter's *The Pursuit of WOW!*
(Vantage, 1994).

· 1048 ·

Always compliment flower gardens and new babies.

· 1049 ·

Remember that it's better to be cheated
in price than in quality.

· 1050 ·

When reading self-help books, include the Bible.

· 1051 ·

Each year, take a first-day-of-school
photograph of your children.

· 1052 ·

Learn the rules of any sport your children play.

· 1053 ·

When you hear a kind word spoken about a friend,
tell him or her so.

· 1054 ·

Never hesitate to do what you know is right.

· 1055 ·

Pack a couple of Ziploc bags and a pad of
Post-it Notes when you travel.

· 1056 ·

Don't work for recognition, but do
work worthy of recognition.

· 1057 ·

Share your knowledge and experiences.

· 1058 ·

Be charitable in your speech, actions,
and judgment.

· 1059 ·

Work for a company where the
expectations of you are high.

· 1060 ·

Don't allow your children or grandchildren
to call you by your first name.

· 1061 ·

Remember that a kind word goes a long way.

· 1062 ·

Don't compare your children with their
siblings or classmates.

· 1063 ·

Be enthusiastic in your expressions of
gratitude and appreciation.

· 1064 ·

Ask permission before taking someone's photograph.

· 1065 ·

Join the Rotary or another civic club.

· 1066 ·

When no great harm will result, let your children
do it their way, even if you know they are wrong.
They will learn more from their mistakes
than from their successes.

· 1067 ·

Forgive quickly.

· 1068 ·

Kiss slowly.

· 1069 ·

Tell your wife often how terrific she looks.

· 1070 ·

Never give an anniversary gift that has to be plugged in.

· 1071 ·

Take some silly photos of yourself and
a friend in an instant photo booth.

· 1072 ·

Remember that regardless of where you are,
not much good happens after midnight.

· 1073 ·

Volunteer to be a Little League umpire.

· 1074 ·

Remember that the word *discipline*
means "to teach."

· 1075 ·

Remember that all success comes at a price.

· 1076 ·

When you give someone a camera as a gift,
make sure it's loaded with film and has a battery.

· 1077 ·

Tour your state capitol building.

· 1078 ·

Own your own tuxedo.

· 1079 ·

Never say anything uncomplimentary about your wife
in the presence of your children.

· 1080 ·

Remember the three universal healers:
calamine lotion, warm oatmeal, and hugs.

· 1081 ·

Earn your success based
on service to others, not
at the expense of others.

· 1082 ·

Kiss your children good night,
even if they are already asleep.

· 1083 ·

To fight the blues, try exercising.

· 1084 ·

Never watch a movie or video with your children
that involves activities and language that you
don't want them to imitate.

· 1085 ·

Learn the Heimlich maneuver.

· 1086 ·

Compliment the parent when you
observe a well-behaved child.

· 1087 ·

When traveling, sleep with your wallet,
car keys, room key, eyeglasses, and shoes nearby.

· 1088 ·

Spend twice as much time praising as
you do criticizing.

· 1089 ·

Never pass up a chance to be in a parade.

· 1090 ·

Start the standing ovation at the end of school plays.

· 1091 ·

Remember the credo of Walt Disney:
Think. Believe. Dream. Dare.

· 1092 ·

When someone lets you down,
don't give up on them.

· 1093 ·

Treat your company's money as you
would your own.

· 1094 ·

Remember that life's big changes rarely
give advance warning.

· 1095 ·

Teach your children never to underestimate
someone with a disability.

· 1096 ·

What you have to do, do wholeheartedly.

· 1097 ·

Never comment on someone's weight unless
you know it's what they want to hear.

· 1098 ·

Read the *Wall Street Journal* regularly.

· 1099 ·

Find a job you love and give it everything you've got.

· 1100 ·

Set limits on the amount and content
of television your children watch.

· 1101 ·

Never complain about a flight delayed
for mechanical repairs. Waiting on the ground is
infinitely better than the alternative.

· 1102 ·

Make a list of travel necessities, laminate it,
and keep it in your suitcase.

· 1103 ·

Keep good financial records.

· 1104 ·

Seek respect rather than popularity.

· 1105 ·

Seek quality rather than luxury.

· 1106 ·

Seek refinement rather than fashion.

· 1107 ·

Never forget that it takes only one person
or one idea to change your life forever.

· 1108 ·

Don't hand out your troubles to
your friends and co-workers.

· 1109 ·

Occasionally let your children help you,
even if it slows you down.

· 1110 ·

Throw a surprise birthday party for a friend.

· 1111 ·

Always take your vacation time.

· 1112 ·

Call (800) 525-9000 for a catalog of Nightingale Conant
tapes on personal development and achievement.

· 1113 ·

Start a "smile file" of jokes, articles, and cartoons
that make you laugh.

· 1114 ·

Start a "read again file" for articles you might want
to enjoy a second time.

· 1115 ·

When you need a little advice, call your grandparents.

· 1116 ·

Teach your sons as well as your daughters
to cook.

· 1117 ·

Report unethical business practices to
your city's Better Business Bureau.

· 1118 ·

Look for the opportunity that's hidden
in every adversity.

· 1119 ·

Remember that when
your mom says,
"You'll regret it,"
you probably will.

· 1120 ·

Don't be critical of your wife's friends.

· 1121 ·

Be prompt when picking up or dropping
off your children for school or other activities.

· 1122 ·

Don't sit while ladies are standing.

· 1123 ·

Take your teenagers with you when you
buy a car or expensive household item
and let them learn from the experience.

· 1124 ·

Become a serious student of American history.

· 1125 ·

Make a big batch of Rice Krispies
squares. Take them to the office.

· 1126 ·

Play catch with a kid.

· 1127 ·

Write some poetry.

· 1128 ·

Shoot a few hoops.

· 1129 ·

Once a month invite someone to lunch who knows
more about your business than you.

· 1130 ·

Never ignore an old barking dog.

· 1131 ·

To open a bottle of champagne,
twist the neck, not the cork.

· 1132 ·

To put someone in your debt, do something
nice for their child.

· 1133 ·

Improve even the best sausage biscuit by spreading
on a little grape jelly.

· 1134 ·

Try to add a new name to your Rolodex every week.

· 1135 ·

If you are not going to use a discount coupon,
leave it on the shelf with the product
for someone else to use.

· 1136 ·

Respect your elders.

· 1137 ·

Never criticize your country when traveling abroad.

· 1138 ·

When loved ones drive away, watch and wave
until you can no longer see the car.

· 1139 ·

On your birthday, send your mom a thank-you card.

· 1140 ·

Never tell an off-color joke in the
presence of women or children.

· 1141 ·

Keep a pad and pencil by every phone.

· 1142 ·

If you dial a wrong number, don't just hang up;
offer an apology.

· 1143 ·

Spend a couple of hours each week reading magazines
that have nothing to do with your job or lifestyle.

· 1144 ·

Hold yourself to the same high standards that you
require of others.

· 1145 ·

Never let the odds keep
you from pursuing what
you know in your heart
you were meant to do.

· 1146 ·

Wage war against procrastination.

· 1147 ·

Don't open anyone else's mail.

· 1148 ·

If you are a guest at a wedding, take lots
of snapshots and send them along with
the negatives to the bride and groom
as quickly as you can. They have a long time
to wait for the formal pictures and will be
thrilled to receive the ones you took.

· 1149 ·

Never loan your chain saw, your ball glove,
or your favorite book.

· 1150 ·

Type out your favorite quotation and
place it where you can see it every day.

· 1151 ·

When playing a sport with a partner,
never criticize his or her performance.

· 1152 ·

Until your children move out of your house,
don't buy anything suede.

· 1153 ·

When the best in the world visits your town
for a concert, exhibition, or speech,
get tickets to attend.

· 1154 ·

Learn the techniques of being a good interviewer.

· 1155 ·

Listen to rumors, but don't contribute
any of your own.

· 1156 ·

When you need to apologize to someone,
do it in person.

· 1157 ·

Offer hope.

· 1158 ·

Let your word be your bond.

· 1159 ·

Count your change.

· 1160 ·

Remember that a lasting marriage is built
on commitment, not convenience.

· 1161 ·

Enter something in the state fair.

· 1162 ·

Try to find a copy of the book *Under My
Elm* by David Grayson (Doubleday, 1942).
You might have to order it.

· 1163 ·

Take your child on a tour of a local university.

· 1164 ·

Finish projects before they are due.

· 1165 ·

Never ask a childless couple when they are
going to have children.

· 1166 ·

Be happy with what you have while working for what you want.

· 1167 ·

Let your children observe your being generous
to those in need.

· 1168 ·

Celebrate even small victories.

· 1169 ·

Never answer a reporter's questions with,
"No comment." Say instead, "I don't have enough
information to comment on that right now."

· 1170 ·

Cut your toenails in private.

· 1171 ·

After going to bed, refuse to worry about
problems until the morning.

· 1172 ·

Return shopping carts to the designated areas.

· 1173 ·

Attend an Eagle Scout's or a Girl Scout's
Golden Award induction ceremony.

· 1174 ·

Never tell a car salesman how much
you want to spend.

· 1175 ·

Redeem gift certificates promptly.

· 1176 ·

Remember that a grateful heart is almost
always a happy one.

· 1177 ·

Make every effort to attend weddings and funerals.

· 1178 ·

Don't forget that a couple of words of praise or
encouragement can make someone's day.

· 1179 ·

Every year, send your old alma mater a few bucks.

· 1180 ·

Be especially courteous to receptionists and secretaries;
they are the gate-keepers.

· 1181 ·

Make your money before spending it.

· 1182 ·

Don't overschedule your children's
extracurricular activities.

· 1183 ·

Whenever you hear an ambulance siren,
say a prayer for the person inside.

· 1184 ·

Worry about the consequences of the choices
you make before you make them—not afterward.

· 1185 ·

Attend parent-teacher conferences
and PTA meetings.

· 1186 ·

Don't take medicine in the dark.

· 1187 ·

Spoil your wife,
not your children.

· 1188 ·

Stop and look up when anyone
approaches your desk.

· 1189 ·

Search out good values, but let the other guy
make a fair profit on what you purchase.

· 1190 ·

Keep a roll of duct tape at home, at
the office, and in your car.

· 1191 ·

Never pass up a chance to jump on a trampoline.

· 1192 ·

Be cautious of renting lodging accommodations
described in the ad or brochure as "rustic."

· 1193 ·

Insist that your children complete a
driver's education course at their school.

· 1194 ·

Locate the emergency exits on your floor as soon as
you check into your hotel room.

· 1195 ·

Get to know your children's teachers.

· 1196 ·

Stay humble.

· 1197 ·

Stay on your toes.

· 1198 ·

Know where to find a gas station that's open
twenty-four hours with a working bathroom.

· 1199 ·

Hang up on anyone you don't know
who's trying to sell you a financial
product over the telephone.

· 1200 ·

Buy each of your children a special Christmas
ornament every year. When they move into
their own homes, box up the ornaments and
give them as house-warming gifts.

· 1201 ·

Support your local museums.

· 1202 ·

Support your local symphony.

· 1203 ·

Support your community college.

· 1204 ·

Remember that you can
miss a lot of good things
in life by having the
wrong attitude.

· 1205 ·

When a guest, never complain about
the food, drink, or accommodations.

· 1206 ·

Take a course in public speaking.

· 1207 ·

Write a letter to the editor at least once a year.

· 1208 ·

For better security when traveling, take along a
small wedge of wood and jam it
under your hotel room door.

· 1209 ·

Never criticize a gift.

· 1210 ·

Never leave a loved one in anger.

· 1211 ·

Get a passport and keep it current.

· 1212 ·

Require your children to do their share
of household chores.

· 1213 ·

When in doubt, smile.

· 1214 ·

Underestimate when guessing an
adult's age or weight.

· 1215 ·

Overestimate when guessing someone's salary.

· 1216 ·

Choose a clothing salesperson who
dresses as you wish you did.

· 1217 ·

Send notes of encouragement to
military personnel and college students.

· 1218 ·

Occasionally leave a quarter in the change return slot
of a pay phone. Somebody always checks.

· 1219 ·

Overpay the neighborhood kid who
does yard work for you.

· 1220 ·

When a friend is in need, help him
without his having to ask.

· 1221 ·

Keep an empty gas can in your trunk.

· 1222 ·

Own a salad spinner.

· 1223 ·

Own two crystal champagne glasses.

· 1224 ·

Allow drivers from out of state a little extra room
on the road.

· 1225 ·

When serving hamburgers, always toast the buns.

· 1226 ·

Never whittle toward yourself.

· 1227 ·

Make a generous contribution
to diabetes research.

· 1228 ·

Teach your children the pride, satisfaction,
and dignity of doing any job well.

· 1229 ·

Never ask a woman
when the baby is due
unless you know
for sure that she's pregnant.

· 1230 ·

Frame anything your child brings home on
his first day of school.

· 1231 ·

Host a backyard get-together for friends
and neighbors every Labor Day.

· 1232 ·

Keep $10 in your glove box for emergencies.

· 1233 ·

Volunteer to help at your city's Special Olympics.

· 1234 ·

Never be too busy
to meet someone new.

· 1235 ·

Remember that cruel words deeply hurt.

· 1236 ·

Remember that loving words quickly heal.

· 1237 ·

Surprise someone who's more than
eighty years old or a couple celebrating
fifty years or more of marriage with a
personal greeting from the President.
Mail details to The White House, Greetings Office,
Room 39, Washington, DC 20500,
four to six weeks in advance.

· 1238 ·

If it's not a beautiful morning, let your cheerfulness make it one.

· 1239 ·

Plant a tree the day your child is born.

· 1240 ·

Toss in a coin when passing a wishing well.

· 1241 ·

Don't say anything on a cordless or cellular telephone that you don't want the world to hear.

· 1242 ·

Never get yourself into a position
where you have to back up a trailer.

· 1243 ·

Marry someone your equal or
a little bit better.

· 1244 ·

Keep a special notebook.
Every night before going to bed,
make a note of something beautiful
that you saw during the day.

· 1245 ·

When you're the first one up, be quiet about it.

· 1246 ·

This year, visit two or three of your
state parks.

· 1247 ·

Remember that a minute of anger
denies you sixty seconds of happiness.

· 1248 ·

Include a recent family photo when
writing to a loved one.

· 1249 ·

Ask your grandparents to tell you stories about
your parents while they were growing up.

· 1250 ·

Become a Big Brother or Big Sister.

· 1251 ·

Welcome the unexpected! Opportunities rarely
come in neat, predictable packages.

· 1252 ·

Before criticizing a new employee, remember
your first days at work.

· 1253 ·

To help your children
turn out well, spend
twice as much time with
them and half as much
money.

· 1254 ·

Take advantage of free lectures on any subject
in which you are remotely interested.

· 1255 ·

Tell family members you love them
before they go away for a few days.

· 1256 ·

Keep a backup copy of your personal
address book.

· 1257 ·

Fill out customer comment cards.

· 1258 ·

Mail in your Publishers Clearing House sweepstakes
notice. Who knows?

· 1259 ·

Don't make eating everything on their plate
an issue with children.

· 1260 ·

Never miss an opportunity to go
fishing with your father.

· 1261 ·

Never miss an opportunity to go
traveling with your mother.

· 1262 ·

Hold a child's hand when crossing the street.

· 1263 ·

Do something every day that maintains
your good health.

· 1264 ·

Every spring set out a couple of tomato plants.

· 1265 ·

When traveling, stop occasionally at
local cafés and diners.

· 1266 ·

Never deny anyone the opportunity to
do something nice for you.

· 1267 ·

Never tell a woman you liked her hair better
before she had it cut.

· 1268 ·

When playing golf and tennis, occasionally play with
someone better than you are.

· 1269 ·

Dust, then vacuum.

· 1270 ·

Offer to pay for parking and tolls when you
ride with someone.

· 1271 ·

Offer to leave the tip when someone
invites you out to eat.

· 1272 ·

Visit a pet store every once in a while and
watch the children watch the animals.

· 1273 ·

Remember that a successful future begins right now.

· 1274 ·

Don't minimize
your child's worries and fears.

· 1275 ·

Give young children the opportunity to participate
in family decision-making. Their insight will
surprise you.

· 1276 ·

Never give up on a dream just because
of the length of time it will take to accomplish it.
The time will pass anyway.

· 1277 ·

Use good stationery when you want your written
comments to be taken seriously.

· 1278 ·

Unless it creates a safety problem,
pull your car over and stop
when a funeral procession is passing.

· 1279 ·

Be the first adult to jump into the pool
or run into the ocean with the kids.
They will love you for it.

· 1280 ·

Hold puppies, kittens, and babies any time you get the chance.

· 1281 ·

When traveling, pack more underwear and socks
than you think you will need.

· 1282 ·

Don't play your car stereo so loud that
you can't hear approaching emergency vehicles.

· 1283 ·

Memorize the names of the books of the Bible.

· 1284 ·

Memorize the names and order
of the Presidents.

· 1285 ·

Take Trivial Pursuit cards to read
to the driver on a long road trip.
It makes the time fly.

· 1286 ·

After children argue and have apologized,
ask each one to say something
nice about the other.

· 1287 ·

Never forget the debt you owe to all
those who have come before you.

· 1288 ·

Watch your back.

· 1289 ·

Watch your weight.

· 1290 ·

Watch your language.

· 1291 ·

Remember that anything creative and innovative
will be copied.

· 1292 ·

Ask your boss what he expects of you.

· 1293 ·

Dress for the position you want, not the one you have.

· 1294 ·

Keep a couple of your favorite inspirational books
by your bedside.

· 1295 ·

Don't write down anything you don't want
someone else to read.

· 1296 ·

Whisper in your sleeping child's ear,
"I love you."

· 1297 ·

At least once in your life,
see the Grand Teton Mountains
from the back of a horse.

· 1298 ·

Never ignore a ringing fire alarm.

· 1299 ·

When taking a true-false test,
remember that any statement that includes
the word *any, all, always, never,* or *ever*
is usually false.

· 1300 ·

Let your children know that regardless of what happens,
you'll always be there for them.

· 1301 ·

Keep a blanket in the trunk of your car for emergencies
during the winter months.

· 1302 ·

Take a ride in a glider.

· 1303 ·

Take a ride in a hot-air balloon.

· 1304 ·

Be the first to apologize to a family member
after a disagreement.

· 1305 ·

To find out who is behind an idea or activity,
follow the money.

· 1306 ·

If you borrow something more than
twice, buy one for yourself.

· 1307 ·

When you build a home, make sure it has a
screened-in porch and a fireplace in the bedroom.

· 1308 ·

Be innovative.

· 1309 ·

Be passionate.

· 1310 ·

Be committed.

· 1311 ·

Become knowledgeable about antiques, oriental rugs,
and contemporary art.

· 1312 ·

Clear the adding machine after using it.

· 1313 ·

Remember that life's
most treasured moments
often come unannounced.

· 1314 ·

Never tell anybody they can't sing.

· 1315 ·

Never tell anybody they don't have
a sense of humor.

· 1316 ·

Call a radio talk show with an opinion.

· 1317 ·

When parents introduce you to their children, say,
"I have looked forward to meeting you,
because your parents are always bragging about you."

· 1318 ·

Don't argue with your mother.

· 1319 ·

Don't get caught glancing at your
watch when you're talking to someone.

· 1320 ·

Before buying that all-important engagement ring,
find out all you can about diamonds
by calling (800) 340-3028.
The American Gem Society will send you
a booklet that will answer
some of your questions.

· 1321 ·

Every December, give the world a precious gift.
Give a pint of blood.

· 1322 ·

Plant a couple of fruit trees in your
back yard.

· 1323 ·

Wear a tie with cartoon characters on
it if you work with kids.

· 1324 ·

Remember that every age brings new opportunities.

· 1325 ·

Know your children's friends.

· 1326 ·

Eat lightly or not at all before giving a speech
or making a presentation.

· 1327 ·

Attend family reunions and be patient when
aunts and uncles want to take your picture.

· 1328 ·

Go for long, hand-holding walks with your wife.

· 1329 ·

Visit the Biltmore estate in Asheville, North Carolina,
during the spring tulip festival.

· 1330 ·

Ask an older person you respect to tell you
his or her proudest moment
and greatest regret.

· 1331 ·

Record the birthday heights
of your children on the kitchen doorjamb.
Never paint it.

· 1332 ·

Every once in a while, let your kids play in the rain.

· 1333 ·

When a woman is in the hospital, give her a soft,
stuffed animal instead of flowers.

· 1334 ·

Always order bread pudding when it's
on the menu.

· 1335 ·

Create and maintain a peaceful home.

· 1336 ·

Become the world's most thoughtful friend.

· 1337 ·

Never ask anyone
why they wear a Medic Alert bracelet.
That's his or her business.

· 1338 ·

Tell gardeners of public areas
how much you appreciate the beauty
they bring to your city.

· 1339 ·

When taking family photos, include
a few routine, everyday shots.

· 1340 ·

Remember that anything worth doing
is going to take longer than you think.

· 1341 ·

No matter how angry you get with your wife,
never sleep apart.

· 1342 ·

Carry a kite in the trunk for windy spring days.

· 1343 ·

Buy a flashlight for each person in
your family to keep in their bedroom.

· 1344 ·

Never marry someone
in hopes that they'll change later.

· 1345 ·

Own a world globe.

· 1346 ·

Own a good set of encyclopedia.

· 1347 ·

Teach a Sunday school class.

· 1348 ·

Never call anybody stupid, even if you're kidding.

· 1349 ·

Find something that's important to your company
and learn to do it better than anyone else.

· 1350 ·

Don't eat anything covered with
chocolate unless you know what's inside.

· 1351 ·

Don't eat anything covered with gravy unless you
know what's under it.

· 1352 ·

Don't drink anything blue.

· 1353 ·

Even when traveling on vacation,
always pack a white dress shirt and a tie.

· 1354 ·

Keep a photograph of each person you have dated.

· 1355 ·

Keep a current city and state highway map
in your car's glove box.

· 1356 ·

Buy your mom flowers and your dad a
new tie with your first paycheck.

· 1357 ·

Be prudent.

· 1358 ·

Be positive.

· 1359 ·

Be polite.

· 1360 ·

Ever wonder what it takes to become an astronaut?
Receive the application package by writing to NASA,
Johnson Space Center, Attn: AHX Astronaut Selection
Office, Houston, TX 77059.

· 1361 ·

If you live in the same city as your mother-in-law,
occasionally trim her hedges and wash her car.

· 1362 ·

Don't buy cheap picture frames.

· 1363 ·

Don't buy a cheap tennis racket.

· 1364 ·

Don't buy a cheap motorcycle helmet.

· 1365 ·

Criticize the behavior, not the person.

· 1366 ·

Never leave fun to find fun.

· 1367 ·

When traveling, carry the phone
number and address of your
destination in your wallet.

· 1368 ·

Collect seashells from your favorite beach.

· 1369 ·

Collect menus from your favorite restaurants.

· 1370 ·

Rebuild a broken relationship.

· 1371 ·

Notify the manager when a restaurant's
restroom isn't clean.

· 1372 ·

On long-distance road trips,
make sure that someone besides the
driver stays awake.

· 1373 ·

Treat yourself
to a professional shoeshine
the next time you're at the airport.

· 1374 ·

At least once a month, get real dirty and sweaty.

· 1375 ·

Ask your child to read a bedtime story
to you for a change.

· 1376 ·

Play Monopoly with your in-laws.
It will reveal a lot about them.

· 1377 ·

Give a trusted auto technician all your repairs,
not just the tough ones.

· 1378 ·

Write a letter of encouragement
to the President—even if he didn't get
your vote.

· 1379 ·

Find a creative florist
and give them all your business.

· 1380 ·

Buy an inexpensive Polaroid camera.
Sometimes you don't want to wait even an hour
to see the pictures.

· 1381 ·

Send Valentines to your children as well as to your wife.

· 1382 ·

When eating cinnamon rolls or prime rib,
eat the center portion first.

· 1383 ·

Add postscripts to your letters.
Make them sweet and kind.

· 1384 ·

Remember that bad luck as well as
good luck seldom lasts long.

· 1385 ·

Never let anyone challenge you to
drive faster than you think is safe.

· 1386 ·

Stop at the visitor's information center when
entering a state for the first time.

· 1387 ·

When you see someone sitting alone
on a bench, make it a point to speak to them.

· 1388 ·

Keep receipts.

· 1389 ·

Wet your hands before lifting a trout from a river.

· 1390 ·

Don't force machinery.

· 1391 ·

When walking a dog,
let the dog pick the direction.

· 1392 ·

Teach your children that when they divide something,
the other person gets first pick of the two pieces.

· 1393 ·

Offer your place in line at the grocery checkout
if the person behind you
has only two or three items.

· 1394 ·

Never give a friend's or relative's
name or phone number
to a telephone solicitor.

· 1395 ·

When going to buy a car, leave your
good watch at home.

· 1396 ·

Don't be so open-minded
that your brains fall out.

· 1397 ·

Learn to make corn bread in a cast-iron skillet.

· 1398 ·

Stand up when an elderly person enters the room.

· 1399 ·

Put a love note in your wife's luggage
before she leaves on a trip.

· 1400 ·

Exercise caution the first
day you buy a chain saw.
You'll be tempted to
cut down everything in
the neighborhood.

· 1401 ·

Never buy an article of clothing thinking it will
fit if you lose a couple of pounds.

· 1402 ·

Root for your team to win,
not for the other team to lose.

· 1403 ·

This year, buy an extra box of Girl Scout cookies.

· 1404 ·

Be grateful that God doesn't answer all your prayers.

· 1405 ·

Accept triumph and defeat with equal grace.

· 1406 ·

Always watch the high school bands' halftime
performances. They practiced just as hard as
the football players.

· 1407 ·

Never set a drink down on a book.

· 1408 ·

Eat at a truck stop.

· 1409 ·

Listen to your favorite music while working
on your tax return.

· 1410 ·

Sniff an open bottle of suntan lotion
and a fresh lime to temporarily curb the winter blues.

· 1411 ·

Never give a pet as a surprise gift.

· 1412 ·

When a child is selling something for a dime,
give a quarter.

· 1413 ·

Never ignore your car's oil warning light.

· 1414 ·

After someone apologizes to you, don't lecture them.

· 1415 ·

When you move into a new house, plant a rosebush
and put out a new welcome mat to
make it seem like home.

· 1416 ·

Make your wedding anniversary an
all-day celebration.

· 1417 ·

Blow a kiss
when driving away from loved ones.

· 1418 ·

Carry a couple of inexpensive umbrellas
in your car that you can give to people
caught in the rain.

· 1419 ·

Be willing to swap
a temporary inconvenience
for a permanent improvement.

· 1420 ·

When you complete a course,
shake the instructor's hand
and thank him or her.

· 1421 ·

Contribute something to each Salvation Army
kettle you pass during the holidays.

· 1422 ·

Regarding rental property,
remember that an unrented house
is better than a bad tenant.

· 1423 ·

Never order barbecue in a restaurant where all the chairs match.

· 1424 ·

Carry a small Swiss Army knife
on your key chain.

· 1425 ·

When you really like someone, tell them.
Sometimes you only get
one chance.

· 1426 ·

Never make fun of people
who speak broken English.
It means they know another language.

· 1427 ·

When going through the checkout line,
always ask the cashier how she's doing.

· 1428 ·

Take more pictures of people than of places.

· 1429 ·

Learn and use the four-digit extension
to your ZIP code.

· 1430 ·

When you need something done, ask a busy person.

· 1431 ·

Call three friends on Thanksgiving
and tell them how thankful you are
for their friendship.

· 1432 ·

Read acknowledgments, introductions, and
prefaces to books.

· 1433 ·

Never underestimate
the influence of the people
you have allowed into your life.

· 1434 ·

Send a "thinking of you" card to a friend
who's experiencing the anniversary of
the loss of a loved one.

· 1435 ·

Learn your great-grandparents' names
and what they did.

· 1436 ·

Enter a room or meeting like you own the place.

· 1437 ·

Refinish a piece of furniture. Just once.

· 1438 ·

Don't use your teeth to open things.

· 1439 ·

When you are angry with someone,
write a letter telling him or her why
you feel that way—but don't mail it.

· 1440 ·

Occasionally walk through old
cemeteries and read the gravestones.

· 1441 ·

Never keep a free ride waiting.

· 1442 ·

Savor every day.

· 1443 ·

If you ask someone to do something for you,
let them do it their way.

· 1444 ·

Once a year take your boss to lunch.

· 1445 ·

Wave to train engineers.

· 1446 ·

Aspirin is aspirin. Buy the least expensive brand.

· 1447 ·

Protect your enthusiasm from the negativity of others.

· 1448 ·

When visiting state and national parks,
take advantage of tours and lectures
given by park rangers.

· 1449 ·

Call your parents as soon as you return from a long trip.

· 1450 ·

Catch up on the bestsellers by listening
to books on tape in your car.

· 1451 ·

Learn to paddle a canoe.

· 1452 ·

When someone you know is down and out,
mail them a twenty-dollar bill anonymously.

· 1453 ·

Share the remote control.

· 1454 ·

When pouring something from one container to another,
do it over the sink.

· 1455 ·

When visitors ask, be able to recommend
three or four free hometown "must sees."

· 1456 ·

Never go up a ladder with just one nail.

· 1457 ·

Remember the best way to improve
your kids is to improve your marriage.

· 1458 ·

When moving from a house or apartment,
for nostalgia's sake, take a photo of each room
while the furniture is still in place.

· 1459 ·

Stand out from the crowd.

· 1460 ·

Pay attention to pictures of missing children.

· 1461 ·

Once in your life, paint a picture.

· 1462 ·

Never buy a Rolex watch from
someone who is out of breath.

· 1463 ·

Never fry bacon while naked.

· 1464 ·

Never squat with your spurs on.

· 1465 ·

Don't spend lots of time with couples
who criticize each other.

· 1466 ·

Read biographies of successful men and women.

· 1467 ·

Remember,
it's not your job to get people to like you,
it's your job to like people.

· 1468 ·

Offer to say grace at holiday meals.

· 1469 ·

Never miss a chance to shake hands with Santa.

· 1470 ·

When someone gives you something, never say,
"You shouldn't have."

· 1471 ·

Remember that the only dumb question
is the one you wanted to ask but didn't.

· 1472 ·

Watch a video on CPR and emergency first aid
with your family.

· 1473 ·

Ask yourself if what you're doing today is getting you closer to where you want to be tomorrow.

· 1474 ·

When you find a coin on the ground,
pick it up and give it
to the first person you see.

· 1475 ·

Add *The Book of Virtues* by William Bennett
(Simon & Schuster, 1993)
to your home library.

· 1476 ·

Don't expect different results
from the same behavior.

· 1477 ·

Spend time with lucky people.

· 1478 ·

Hug a cow.

· 1479 ·

Make your bed every morning.

· 1480 ·

Wash whites separately.

· 1481 ·

Keep a couple of Wet-Naps in the glove box.

· 1482 ·

Never date anyone who has more than two cats.

· 1483 ·

Treat your parents
to a dinner out on your birthday.

· 1484 ·

Don't look through other people's medicine cabinets,
closets, or refrigerators.

· 1485 ·

Always offer guests something to eat or drink
when they drop by.

· 1486 ·

When someone tells you they love you, never say,
"No, you don't."

· 1487

When you race your kids,
let them win at the end.

· 1488 ·

Once a summer, run through a yard sprinkler.

· 1489 ·

For an unforgettable adventure,
float the Gauley River in West Virginia.

· 1490 ·

Remember that nothing important was ever achieved
without someone's taking a chance.

· 1491 ·

Stand up for your high principles even
if you have to stand alone.

· 1492 ·

Watch reruns of *The Wonder Years*.

· 1493 ·

Every couple of months, spend thirty minutes
or so in a big toy store.

· 1494 ·

Never resist
a generous impulse.

· 1495 ·

When babies are born into your family,
save the newspaper from that day.
Give it to them on their eighteenth birthday.

· 1496 ·

Support family-run businesses.

· 1497 ·

Carefully examine your written work
when you are finished.

· 1498 ·

Be faithful.

· 1499 ·

Write a thank-you note to your
children's teacher when you see your
child learning new things.

· 1500 ·

When on vacation or a family holiday,
don't be too concerned about the cost.
This is not a time to count pennies;
it's a time to make memories.

· 1501 ·

Even on short ferry rides, always get
out of your car and enjoy the crossing.

· 1502 ·

Read the *Old Farmer's Almanac.*

· 1503 ·

Remember that everyone has bad days.

· 1504 ·

Learn to eat with chopsticks.

· 1505 ·

Make sure the telephone number on your letterhead
and business card is large enough to be read easily.

· 1506 ·

Never sharpen a boomerang.

· 1507 ·

Never intentionally embarrass anyone.

· 1508 ·

Question your prejudices.

· 1509 ·

Eat moderately.

· 1510 ·

Exercise vigorously.

· 1511 ·

When you're angry, take a thirty-minute walk;
when you're really angry, chop some firewood.

· 1512 ·

Be wary of stopping at restaurants displaying
Help Wanted signs.

· 1513 ·

When returning a book
or an item of clothing you have borrowed,
leave a note of appreciation.

· 1514 ·

When you pass a family riding in a big U-Haul truck,
give them the "thumbs-up" sign. They need all the
encouragement they can get.

· 1515 ·

Have your piano tuned every six months.

· 1516 ·

Avoid automated teller machines
at night.

· 1517 ·

Add *Art of the Western World* to your
videocassette collection.

· 1518 ·

Remember the main thing is to keep
the main thing the main thing.

· 1519 ·

Have your pastor over for dinner.

· 1520 ·

Marry someone who loves music.

· 1521 ·

Learn the history of your hometown.

· 1522 ·

Take your family to a dude ranch for a vacation.

· 1523 ·

See any detour as an opportunity to
experience new things.

· 1524 ·

When adults are sick, care for them as
though they were children.

· 1525 ·

Watch what you eat at cocktail parties.
Each hors d'oeuvre has
about one hundred calories.

· 1526 ·

Remember that wealth is not
having all the money you want,
but having all the money you need.

· 1527 ·

When deplaning, thank the captain for
a safe and comfortable flight.

· 1528 ·

Never break off communications with your children,
no matter what they do.

· 1529 ·

Have a little money in the bank to
handle unforeseen problems.

· 1530 ·

Read *Growing a Business* by Paul Hawken
(Simon & Schuster, 1987).

· 1531 ·

Remember that much truth is spoken in jest.

· 1532 ·

Don't forget that your attitude is just
as important as the facts.

· 1533 ·

Visit the Art Institute of Chicago.

· 1534 ·

Take a course in basic car repair.

· 1535 ·

Take your dad bowling.

· 1536 ·

Don't live with the brakes on.

· 1537 ·

Never complain
about the food or entertainment
at church suppers or charity functions.

· 1538 ·

When talking to someone
who's a new parent,
always ask to see a picture of the baby.

· 1539 ·

Remember that true happiness comes
from virtuous living.

· 1540 ·

Don't obligate yourself
to a home mortgage larger than
three times your family's annual income.

· 1541 ·

When asked, take the time to give out-of-town visitors
complete and clear directions.

· 1542 ·

Pass down family recipes.

· 1543 ·

Talk to your plants.

· 1544 ·

Ask for advice when you need it, but remember that
no one is an expert on your life.

· 1545 ·

If you know you're going to lose, do it with style.

· 1546 ·

Say something every day that
encourages your children.

· 1547 ·

Rescue your dreams.

· 1548 ·

Remember that creating a successful marriage is like farming; you have to start over again every morning.

· 1549 ·

Teach by example.

· 1550 ·

Commit yourself to a mighty purpose.

· 1551 ·

Live simply.

· 1552 ·

Think quickly.

· 1553 ·

Work diligently.

· 1554 ·

Fight fairly.

· 1555 ·

Give generously.

· 1556 ·

Laugh loudly.

· 1557 ·

Love deeply.

· 1558 ·

Plant more flowers than you pick.

· 1559 ·

Remember that all important truths are simple.

· 1560 ·

Include your parents in your prayers.

Dear Reader,

If you received advice from your parents or grandparents that was especially meaningful and you would like me to share it with other readers, please write and tell me about it.

I look forward to hearing from you.

H. Jackson Brown, Jr.
P.O. Box 150155
Nashville TN 37215